West Academic Publishing's Law School Advisory Board

The MPT

Katherine Silver Kelly

Clinical Professor of Law
The Ohio State University
Moritz College of Law

A SHORT & HAPPY GUIDE® SERIES

WEST
ACADEMIC
PUBLISHING

a short & happy guide series is a trademark registered in the U.S. Patent and Trademark Office.

© 2023 LEG, Inc. d/b/a West Academic
  860 Blue Gentian Road, Suite 350
  Eagan, MN 55121
  1-877-888-1330

Printed in the United States of America

ISBN: 978-1-68561-115-6

Preface

Standard Bar Exam Acronyms

This book is about the Multistate Performance Test, more commonly referred to as the MPT. MPT is just one of many bar exam-related acronyms you will encounter throughout bar prep. Here is a brief overview of the most common bar exam acronyms:

NCBE	National Conference of Bar Examiners	Entity that creates, distributes, manages, and scores the bar exam.
UBE	Uniform Bar Exam	Bar exam administered in 40+ jurisdictions, comprised of the MBE, MEE, and MPT.
MBE	Multistate Bar Exam	200 question multiple choice component of the bar exam, tests substantive law in 7 main subjects, each subject is equally tested.
MEE	Multistate Essay Exam	6 question essay component of the bar exam, tests substantive law from a 12 subject "pool." You don't know what subjects are tested until you get the questions.
MPT	Multistate Performance Test	2 question closed-universe, practical component of the bar exam. No substantive knowledge is required.

| MPRE | Multistate Professional Responsibility Exam | 60 question multiple choice ethics test that is not part of the bar exam but required for licensure 48 jurisdictions. |

Standardized Tests

The purpose of this book is not to defend the standardized test. There is no question that standardized tests like the bar exam tend to be gatekeeping mechanisms that reward those with access to resources and preserve the status quo. However, not everything about a standardized test is bad. The definition of a standardized test is that it is designed, administered, and graded in a "standard" or consistent manner and must be both valid and reliable. A test is valid if it measures what it claims to measure and it is reliable if it produces similar results under consistent conditions from one test to the next (year after year).

Why is this important? It means that for MPT problems to be valid and reliable, they have to follow a design template. Every MPT is created using standard formulas and patterns. MPT problems are not identical but they are the same. Let me say that again: MPTs are not identical but they are the same. MPTs might initially appear different from each other but under the surface they are variations of the same template. Let's compare this to a real world example of driving a car. If you drive a small sedan like a Toyota Corolla, you could easily drive a Honda Civic or a Hyundai Elantra. The cars are not identical and it might take a minute to acquaint yourself with the particulars, but the basic mechanics are the same. MPT problems operate the same way—any differences are simply variations of the same underlying formula.

The basic premise of this book is standardization and how to use it to your advantage. Once you become familiar the standards, no MPT will confuse or surprise you.

- standard formulas on which MPTs are created;

- standard approaches for reading and organizing material;

- standard tools for managing and prioritizing time;

- standard expectations of bar examiners;

- standard strategies for practice and assessment; and

- standard mistakes and misconceptions, and how to avoid them.

How to Use this Book

This book gives concrete and practical advice but it does not contain any actual MPTs. This is because the NCBE owns the rights to all MPT material, regardless of whether it is freely accessible on its website. Licensing fees are expensive and would make this book cost prohibitive. This book is an abstract discussion about the MPT and it is not meant to be read like a novel (one-time read all the way through). This book is a hands-on companion guide and reference tool you should use throughout bar prep alongside MPT problems, point sheets, and sample responses from the NCBE website or your commercial bar prep company.

Katherine Silver Kelly

December, 2022

Table of Contents

A Short & Happy Guide to
the MPT

CHAPTER 1

Standard Testing Basics

A. MPT Overview and Skills Tested

The MPT is a closed universe test of practical writing skills created by the National Conference of Bar Examiners (NCBE). Every UBE jurisdiction uses the MPT as do many non-UBE jurisdictions. According to the NCBE:

> The MPT is designed to test an examinee's ability to use fundamental lawyering skills in a realistic situation and complete a task that a beginning lawyer should be able to accomplish. The MPT is not a test of substantive knowledge. Rather, it is designed to evaluate certain fundamental skills lawyers are expected to demonstrate regardless of the area of law in which the skills are applied.[1]

In other words, the MPT is not simply a writing test, it is a skills test. The NCBE identifies six skills as:[2]

---

[1] *See* National Conference of Bar Examiners, https://www.ncbex.org/exams/mpt/ (last visited June 30, 2022).

[2] *See* National Conference of Bar Examiners, https://www.ncbex.org/exams/mpt/preparing/ (last visited June 30, 2022).

(1) sort detailed factual materials and separate relevant from irrelevant facts; (2) analyze statutory, case, and administrative materials for applicable principles of law; (3) apply the relevant law to the relevant facts in a manner likely to resolve a client's problem; (4) identify and resolve ethical dilemmas, when present; (5) communicate effectively in writing; and (6) complete a lawyering task within time constraints.

These skills fall into two basic categories: competency and professionalism.

The competency skills are:

- problem solving—Identify and resolve the legal issues presented by the law and facts. Do not speculate or offer advice beyond the material provided.

- legal analysis and reasoning—explain how legal principles operate and engage in the appropriate depth of analysis.

- factual analysis—Explain how specific facts connect to law and use analogical reasoning to compare or distinguish precedent case facts.

The professionalism skills are:

- written communication—be precise yet complete, use professional writing practices like CREAC, paragraphing, topic sentences, transition phrases, etc.

- organization and time management—Follow directions and pay attention to details; use a logical structure; engage in appropriate depth of analysis.

- recognizing and resolving ethical dilemmas—do not misrepresent facts or law as a way to achieve your client's goals or so they can prevail.

As you can see, these are all skills you learned in law school. The MPT tests your ability to think, work, and stay in control under pressure. Because you know what the bar examiners expect, you will practice with this in mind. You will not rush to start writing, nor will you copy giant blocks of information from cases or write your thoughts in stream of consciousness.

B. Points and Grading

In addition to a standardized design, there is standardized grading system for MPTs. Like the other bar exam components, the MPT is anonymously graded. On the UBE, each MPT is worth 10% of your score, 20% overall. Most [3]UBE jurisdictions use a raw score range of 1-6 and multiply that by 2.

The raw score is based on holistic assessment of the response that is relative and curved. The bar examiners do not determine if a response is passing or failing and there is no checklist where you have to get a certain percentage of points to earn a particular score. Instead, the bar examiners use rank order grading and the score assigned depends on how a response compares relative to other responses.

Here is an example of a UBE jurisdiction rank order grading scale that is representative of how bar examiners score MPT responses:[4]

---

[3]   Check your jurisdiction to confirm. For example, New York uses a 20-80 point scale, Missouri uses a 10-point scale.

[4]   *See* Maryland State Board of Law Examiners, https://www.mdcourts.gov/sites/default/files/import/ble/pdfs/gbinformationpacket.pdf (last accessed August 1, 2022).

Score	Description of Demonstrated Performance
6	A **6** answer is a very good answer relative to the sample group of answers. A **6** answer usually indicates that the examinee has a thorough comprehension of the practical and academic aspects of the question, understands and synthesizes the relevant factual and legal materials and uses them to write a legally supported, well-written, responsive product in the time allotted. A **6** should not be reserved for perfect answers, but it should be given to the best answers in the sample group.
5	A **5** answer is an above-average answer relative to the sample group. A **5** answer usually indicates that the examinee has a fairly complete understanding of the practical and academic aspects of the question, understands and synthesizes most of the relevant factual and legal materials, and uses them to write a legally supported, reasonably well-written, mostly responsive product in the time allotted. A **5** answer is among the better answers in the sample group but is not as strong as a **6** answer.
4	A **4** answer is an average answer relative to the sample group. A 4 answer usually indicates that the examinee fairly understands the practical and academic aspects of the question, understands enough of the relevant factual and legal materials to incorporate them into a relatively satisfactory, albeit less than completely responsive product in the time allotted. A **4** answer is among the mid-range of answers in the sample group; it is not as strong as **5** and **6** answers, but better than **1-3** answers.
3	A **3** answer is a somewhat below average answer relative to the sample group. A **3** answer usually indicates that it is, on balance, inadequate. It shows that the examinee has a

Check your specific jurisdiction for additional policies as some permit highlighters, provide ear plugs, or provide scratch paper.

Non-Standard Testing Time

Individuals who receive ADA Accommodations will have different testing times and testing schedule. This depends on the amount of additional time and the jurisdiction. Jurisdictions do not tend to publish non-standard test times on their public websites so contact your jurisdiction directly and ask for the testing schedule.

25%—This is an additional 45 minutes and jurisdictions tend to add that time to the standard testing schedule. You will get both MPTs at once and have 3 hours and 45 minutes to complete the tasks with no break in between MPTs. When you account for the additional 45 minutes added to your essay time, this makes for a long day of testing. Some jurisdictions start earlier than the standard 9-9:30 time so that the exam day does not extend past 6:30pm.

50%—This is an additional 90 minutes and jurisdictions differ in how they administer the exam. Some simply add this time to the standard testing schedule. If that is the case, you would get both MPTs at once and have 4 hours and 30 minutes to complete the tasks with no break. This makes for a long testing day because you will also have 90 minutes added to your essay component.

Some jurisdictions break up the testing and extend it over three days instead of two.

Instead of getting both MPTs at once, you will get one at a time and have 2 hours and 15 minutes to complete it. Below is an example of what a 50% additional time extended testing schedule might look like:

Tuesday AM—MPT 1; Tuesday PM—MPT 2

Wednesday AM—MBE 1-100; Wednesday PM—MBE 101-200

Thursday AM—MEE 1-3; Thursday PM—MEE 4-6

100%—This is an additional 3 hours so you will not get both MPTs at once and be expected to test for 6 hours non-stop. You might have done this for law school exams and think it is manageable for the MPT but don't forget about the essay component. Even the bar examiners are not so unreasonable that they would require you to test for 12 hours (and then have to come back the next day and test for 12 more hours on the MBE). Instead, you will get one MPT at a time and have 3 hours to complete it. Below is an example of what a 100% additional time extended testing schedule might look like:

Tuesday AM—MPT 1; Tuesday PM—MPT 2

Wednesday AM—MBE 1-50; Wednesday PM—MBE 51-100

Thursday AM—MBE 101-150; Thursday PM—MBE 151-200

Friday AM—MEE 1-3; Friday PM—MEE 4-6

Again, jurisdictions differ in how they administer non-standard test conditions and this can change year to year. Contact your jurisdiction to find out what testing schedule you can expect.

CHAPTER 2

Standard MPT Formulas

A. Standard Format and Components

The MPT is developed by the National Conference of Bar Examiners (NCBE). It is a closed-universe task similar to an introductory level assignment you might have had in your first year legal writing class. UBE jurisdictions administer two MPTs and other jurisdictions may choose one or both MPT items. It is administered in the morning of the first day of the bar exam.

At an in-person bar exam, the MPT material is in a paper booklet and you will write[1] or type your response in a separate document. All jurisdictions permit you to bring pens (some allow highlighters) so you can take notes and write anywhere on the test booklet.

---

[1] Recently some jurisdictions have announced they will no longer allow examinees to handwrite the MPT or essay components so if you are a handwriter, check to see if your jurisdiction allows it.

General Instructions

Every MPT has the same instructions on the back cover:[2]

You will be instructed when to begin and when to stop this test. Do not break the seal on this booklet until you are told to begin. This test is designed to evaluate your ability to handle a select number of legal authorities in the context of a factual problem involving a client.

The problem is set in the fictitious state of Franklin, in the fictitious Fifteenth Circuit of the United States. Columbia and Olympia are also fictitious states in the Fifteenth Circuit. In Franklin, the trial court of general jurisdiction is the District Court, the intermediate appellate court is the Court of Appeal, and the highest court is the Supreme Court.

You will have two kinds of materials with which to work: a File and a Library. The first document in the File is a memorandum containing the instructions for the task you are to complete. The other documents in the File contain factual information about your case and may include some facts that are not relevant.

The Library contains the legal authorities needed to complete the task and may also include some authorities that are not relevant. Any cases may be real, modified, or written solely for the purpose of this examination. If the cases appear familiar to you, do not assume that they are precisely the same as you have read before. Read them thoroughly, as if they all were new to you. You should assume that the cases were decided in the jurisdictions and on the dates shown. In citing cases from

---

[2] *See* National Conference of Bar Examiners, https://www.ncbex.org/pdfviewer/?file=%2Fdmsdocument%2F53.

the Library, you may use abbreviations and omit page references.

Your response must be written in the answer book provided. If you are using a laptop computer to answer the questions, your jurisdiction will provide you with specific instructions. In answering this performance test, you should concentrate on the materials in the File and Library. What you have learned in law school and elsewhere provides the general background for analyzing the problem; the File and Library provide the specific materials with which you must work.

Although there are no restrictions on how you apportion your time, you should allocate approximately half your time to reading and digesting the materials and to organizing your answer before you begin writing it. You may make notes anywhere in the test materials; blank pages are provided at the end of the booklet. You may not tear pages from the question booklet.

Do not include your actual name anywhere in the work product required by the task memorandum.

This performance test will be graded on your responsiveness to the instructions regarding the task you are to complete, which are given to you in the first memorandum in the File, and on the content, thoroughness, and organization of your response.

Perhaps you read these instructions carefully but chances are you did a quick skim or skipped it entirely. There is a reason the full instructions are included in the text of this chapter so let's go over a few key details:

Jurisdiction

All MPTs are set in the fictitious state of Franklin the fictitious Fifteenth Circuit. There are two neighboring states, Columbia and Olympia. Franklin has three levels of courts: trial, appellate, and supreme. The trial court is the district court, appellate court is called the court of appeal. The state courts all fall within the jurisdiction of the real Supreme Court of the United States.

You are probably thinking, "it's a fictitious jurisdiction, what more do I need to understand?" A fictitious jurisdiction is part of what standardizes the MPT. Except for Supreme Court of the United States cases, the case law is made up and does not reflect the rules from any one jurisdiction. This is especially important if the legal issue(s) is one you are familiar with. Do not assume you know rules and therefore do not need to read the legal authority closely. Do not jump to the conclusion that familiarity with a legal issue means you do not have to spend as much time reading and organizing. In fact, there is a specific instruction cautioning against this: "if the cases seem familiar to you, do not assume that they are precisely the same as you have read before. Read them thoroughly, as if they all were new to you."

Ignore this instruction at your own peril. Remember, the MPT is a skills test, and one of those skills is to read and analyze legal authorities. The only way to standardize this skill so examinees are not advantaged or disadvantaged based on familiarity with the subject matter is to tweak the legal standards, rule components, tests, and terminology. Do not substitute your personal assumptions for the drafters' instructions but also do not overthink it and assume that all the rules are different from what you may have learned. As discussed in Chapter 9, the purpose of the MPT is not to trick people and the best approach is a reasonable one.

MPT Material

The MPT is divided into two sections—the file and the library. The file contains all the factual information you need and it is either instructional or evidentiary. The library contains all relevant legal authority such as statutes, regulations, treatises, and cases.

File Material

Knowing the file material is either instructional or evidentiary allows you to assign meaning to the documents ahead of time instead of trying to figure it out as you are reading them. Instructional file material includes the task memo and, depending on the task, a supplemental format document. The task memo is arguably the most important document in the MPT and we will go in depth on how to use it in the next section.

Evidentiary file documents are the substantive facts you will use in your analysis. Unless otherwise instructed, treat all facts and file information as admissible. These documents are usually organized in order of the legal issues and although every document is relevant to the analysis, you will not use them equally or in the same way.

Evidentiary documents can be either primary or supporting. Primary documents are relevant to the legal analysis and supporting documents are relevant to task completion.

Examples of primary documents include:

Interviews—clients, witnesses

Depositions, affidavits, court filings

Public information—news stories, commercials, social media

Communications—emails, letters from client or opposing counsel

Reports—police investigations, recommendations, internal reviews

Examples of supporting documents and how to use them:

Standard Forms—example document to use as starting point when task is to draft an agreement or contract.

Legal Summaries—background information to assist understanding of legal issues and how to interpret. This helps standardize the test so that no one has an advantage of being more familiar with a particular legal concept.

Factual Summaries—summary of similar cases and outcomes (ex: jury verdicts) for you to use as basis to support recommendation or position.

Although all file documents are generally factual, each serves a specific purpose and when you know this you can read with this purpose in mind.

Library Material

The library contains all necessary legal authority and is both federal and state material. Although there is not always statutory material, this is a broad term that includes statutes and administrative regulations; evidentiary and procedural rules; rules of professional conduct; and treatises and restatements. Case law includes mandatory authority from Franklin and the Supreme Court of the United States, and persuasive authority from Olympia and Columbia and ethics advisory opinions.

Similar to file documents, every library document is relevant but you will not use every authority equally or in the same way. Also similar to the file is that the material is often organized in the order of the legal issues. If the MPT has statutory authority, it will be the first library document. The cases that follow interpret relevant statutory provisions. Cases work together and a more complex or in-depth issue will have two cases.

Regardless of the type of library material, treat it as law and use it to support your legal reasoning. The general instructions say, "[i]n citing cases from the Library, you may use abbreviations and omit page references." In explaining how to cite cases, the instructions are implicitly telling you that you *should* cite to the legal authority. Even if the individual MPT does not have an explicit instruction to cite library material, you should do it. This makes sure you only use the legal authority provided and it shows the bar examiners that you are using it instead of bringing in outside knowledge.

Grading

The last paragraph of the general instructions lays out the performance expectations for assessment. You are graded on your ability to follow the specific task instructions and execute a document that is both a thorough and organized analysis of the relevant issues. Keep this in mind when we get to Chapter 5 and Standard Timing Tools.

Standard Tasks

There are two types of MPT tasks—predictive and persuasive. A predictive task is one that seeks advice or a recommended course of action. The standard predictive task is the office memo. Variations include an opinion letter, bench memo, or drafting a document. A persuasive task is one that makes an argument or advocates for a certain outcome. The standard persuasive task is the trial brief and variations include a demand letter, opening/closing argument.

I used the term "variations" for a reason. Do not get caught up in the specific types of tasks or the audience. Task titles might not be identical but the only difference between the standard and a variation is the heading that signals the type of document. Although you might adjust the tone slightly, it should always be professional, logical, and clear.

Remember, the MPT is a standardized test that tests the same skills regardless of the specific work product. If the task title is something other than a basic office memo, there is always guidance either in a formatting document or template examples. When you practice MPTs and come across an unfamiliar task title, instead of wasting time and energy trying to figure out what it means, simply categorize it as predictive or persuasive and treat it as a memo or brief. Even if there are specific formatting instructions, they will still follow the standard analytical framework you learned in law school.

By the time you get to the bar exam, you will have practiced enough MPTs such that nothing should throw you off. If you get a task title you have not seen before, do not manufacture a disadvantage that does not exist. Categorize it as predictive or persuasive and move forward.

The Task Memo and Formatting Documents

Every MPT has a task memo with specific instructions for that particular MPT. The task memo is written as instructions from a supervising attorney and it not only tells you what to do, it tells you how to do it. You need to do more than just read it carefully, you should engage with the material and start setting up your organizational framework that will ultimately become your drafted response. Do not rush through the task memo (or other formatting documents) thinking you need to hurry up and get to the facts or rules. Although you have a limited amount of time, you still need to digest and organize the material. Reading speed has nothing to do with reading quality.

This is where standardized test practices come into play. Task memos are based on a standard template with three components: factual overview, legal overview, and organizational overview.

The factual overview introduces the client, factual context, and establishes the type of legal relationship—advisory or advocacy. It is followed by the legal overview which identifies the general issues and structure of analysis. The last component is the organizational overview which contains the task-specific instructions like the work product and audience, it also shows you how to analyze, what order to analyze, and sets task parameters.

Depending on the task, some MPTs include a separate document with detailed formatting instructions. It supplements the task memo and provides the procedural structure such as document components and what order to address them, how to draft headings, etc. It will not include substantive information about the legal issues.

If you read the task memo or format document without keeping in mind the skills the MPT tests and that it is based on a standard formula, you might miss the key details. Key details are often repeated words and phrases that give you organizational signals.

Although the guidance might be implicit, it is not hidden. Examples of key details often appearing in formatting documents:

Brief, succinct, short

Specific, particular, each, individual

Thorough, fully, in depth

You know the meaning of these words and likely notice them when reading MPT task documents. However, these words are so familiar that you also likely skim over them instead of appreciating what they are there to do. The MPT drafters repeat organizational signals to tell you what to do and how to do it. Pay attention to repeated words and similar terminology within the instructions. Determine if it goes to a legal issue, organization, or depth of analysis, and consider the overall context. For example, if the task is a demand letter, you will be instructed to draft a brief introduction, give a succinct factual overview, and thoroughly analyze the facts and applicable law. You have a lot to do in 90 minutes so whenever you see a limiting instruction like "brief," or "succinct," make sure you adhere to it and prioritize your time accordingly.

The standard MPT format is based on 2-3 main legal issues. Regardless of whether they are obvious or more implicit, pay attention and make note of them in the task memo before moving on to other documents. The main issues set up the context for the entire MPT and if you know what these are, you can read the rest of the material much more efficiently.

In addition to context, the main issues also provide key organizational cues—the order in which they are written is the same order you should follow. This allows you to start organizing the document and your thoughts right away and to read the file and library material with a purpose. You must know what you are reading and how to use the information. Take a minute to go through an MPT task memo and identify the main issues and the order in which they are written. The next step is to build an organizational framework.

Building a Standard Organizational Framework

Building an organizational framework means exactly what you think it does. Go beyond passive acknowledgement of information like underlining, circling, brackets etc. Actively engage with the material and pull out what you need to construct a framework that you can add to as you move through the MPT documents. Build one step at a time as you go along instead of trying to remember the information and how it fits together. You are drafting a template that you can fill in instead of creating a complete document from scratch.

Here is an example of a standard organizational framework for any task:

Document Heading

[memo, letter, etc.]

Introduction/Roadmap This is a fairly generic introduction that is easily tailored to almost any task, predictive or persuasive.

Predictive—You asked me to write a memo for the Alexandra McConnell case on whether she can prevail on the claims and recommending a course of action. As detailed below, it appears that McConnell has meritorious claims for assault and battery and should be able to recover both compensatory and punitive damages.

Persuasive—I am writing on behalf of my client Alexandra McConnell regarding the incident with your client. The purpose of this letter is to show that McConnell has meritorious claims for assault and battery and is entitled to sizable compensatory and punitive damages.

Discussion Organize the discussion section using the standard CREXAC/CREAC framework you learned in your first year legal writing course. The framework is the same regardless of whether it is a predictive or persuasive task.

[introduction-conclusion] McConnell has a claim for assault.

[rule, explanation]

[analysis]

[connection-conclusion] In addition to assault, McConnell can also establish battery.

[introduction-conclusion] McConnell has a claim for battery.

[rule, explanation]

[analysis]

[connection-conclusion] Based on her claims for assault and battery, McConnell can recover compensatory and punitive damages.

Conclusion Similar to the introduction, you can use information from the task memo to pre-write a simple conclusion that is easily tailored to any task.

Predictive—In conclusion, there is sufficient evidence to establish the legal claims and the case law indicates she could recover significant damages. As such, I recommend the firm go forward with the case.

Persuasive—The relevant legal authority makes it clear that we have a strong case against your client and it is in their best interest to reach a reasonable settlement.

As you can see, using the task memo to build an organizational framework provides a visible and tangible foundation that you can develop as you go through the MPT. It is standard enough to work with any MPT and easily adaptable to specific legal and factual issues.

CHAPTER 3

Standard Approaches to Reading

A. Determine Your Standard Reading Approach

Once you have built your standard organizational framework from the task memo, the next step is to start filling it in. Just as the task memo is based on a standard template, so is every other document in the MPT. This means you can use a standard approach for reading and organizing the material. Although you might have slight variations, your standard approaches will work for any MPT regardless of the topic or task.

The MPT has two general components—a file and library and you need to determine in what order you want to proceed: "Facts First" or "Lead with the Law."

Facts First

"Facts First" means that you need factual context for reading the law, with an emphasis on "context." It does not mean you pour over every detail or take extensive notes on the file documents. You don't know what factual details are relevant until you know the specific legal components. Spend a maximum of five minutes skimming the file documents, taking few, if any, notes. The goal is to get some factual context and start thinking about potential legal issues. You will come back for the details later.

Once you have a general sense of the factual background, go to the library and read the material with this context in mind, identifying specific legal issues. As you see what legal issues need to be addressed you will continue to build on to the analytical framework you started from the task memo. Then you will go back to the file and, because you are familiar with that material, you know what to look for and where to find it. You can then pull out the relevant facts and connect them to the legal issues.

Lead with the Law

"Lead with the Law" means you go from the task memo to the library and build out your legal framework. You then go through the file documents and identify relevant factual details and where they go in the framework. This approach is similar to preparing and taking a law school exam. The material in the library is like your class notes—it is already organized and needs to be synthesized into a more cohesive structure. The file material is the exam hypo— because you already understand the legal issues and how to analyze them, you recognize legally significant facts as you read them and can include them in the framework.

Determine Which Standard Approach Works Best for You

Do not automatically assume you are a "Facts First" or "Lead with the Law" person but try both to make sure you are choosing the one that works best for you. You might assume you need the factual story in order to understand the legal issues and this might be true for an open research situation. However, the MPT provides the relevant legal authority so it might be better to see what the specific legal issues are so you know what facts to address. On the other hand, you might assume you need to set up an outline to understand the facts. This might be true when you have a semester's worth of material and you have to prepare for any number of factual scenarios. On the MPT the file lays out all the facts so you do not have to guess what issues will be tested. Instead of spending time constructing a detailed outline of every legal issue, perhaps it is better to first get a sense of the factual issues you will analyze.

Over the course of bar prep you will work through several practice MPTs (7-10) and the first few are about familiarizing yourself with the MPT and figuring out your standard approach. Practice both and weigh the pros and cons of each. Once you know what to expect and develop a standard approach, you will feel confident in your abilities and be able to remain calm and stay in control during the exam.

B. Standard Approach to Reading the Library

To determine whether you prefer "Facts First" or "Lead with the Law," it might be helpful to understand the standard format for library material. MPT libraries contain a variety of legal authorities, all of which you have encountered at some point in law school. There is no secret trick to how library material is organized nor is there hidden information. If the library is all case law, keep it simple and read the cases in order. Cases are almost always in the order of the legal issues and how you should organize your analysis. The language is straightforward with headings and organizational signals (ex: the first issue is. . . , the most important factor is. . .). Cases will not contradict each other and are set up to explain how the rules work together. If you look for this, you will find it.

How to Read Statutes

If the library has statutes and cases, the statutes will always be first and at least one of the cases will interpret relevant statutory provisions. Before you read the cases, skim the statutory provisions by reading the headings. This gives you context as statutes set up the structure for case interpretation and much like statutes in real life, they are not necessarily written in the order of analysis. Instead, pay attention to the order in which a case analyzes the statutory provisions as this is the same order you will use for your analysis. Once you see how the cases use that material, you will then go back to the statute and read those provisions. You will also make note of provisions not analyzed in the cases—do not immediately dismiss them, but without case law to interpret, these provisions are not likely relevant or require only a cursory application.

How to Read Cases

The MPT is not a test of substantive law, so cases provide everything you need to resolve the legal issues. Take an active approach instead of a static approach. Do not read cases the same way you did 1L year—from the first word to the last. Instead of reading for static information such as the legal issues and rules, read for the analytical process. Identify the reason the parties are in court, what is being litigated, and how the court resolves the dispute. Pay attention to cues for resolving the dispute such as headings, numbered legal tests, specific statutory provisions, internal case illustrations, order of analysis, and depth of analysis. Similar to the task memo, the key details are there and if you know to look for them, you will find them.

Case Reading Strategies

Resist the urge to immediately start taking notes and copy rules as you come across them. Instead, first read through the entire case to see not only what the rules are but how the court applies them.

The first and last paragraphs give you the "what," "how," and "why." The first paragraph identifies the specific issue and lays out the roadmap for how to analyze it. The last paragraph states the overall conclusion and the main legal reasons for why the court reached this outcome. Taken together, the first and last paragraphs provide a basic framework for organizing and analyzing specific legal issues.

Pay attention to what is *not* discussed in a case. Because you have identified the main legal issues from the task memo, you want to take note of whether a case fully addresses that issue. For example, let's say one of the main legal issues is whether your client committed aggravated assault. The library has a statute and two cases. The statute establishes that a person commits aggravated assault if they intentional cause serious bodily injury. The first case defines serious bodily injury as one that causes a substantial risk of death, serious permanent disfigurement, or protracted loss or impairment. It then analyzes injuries that are substantial risk of death and serious permanent disfigurement. It does not analyze protracted loss or impairment. Not only can you expect the second case to analyze this type of injury but it will likely mean a more in depth analysis than the other types of injuries. This is a signal that the depth of analysis for your issues should be the same.

C. How to Read the File

Although the MPT is supposed to simulate real world tasks a beginning attorney might encounter, you will not have to sift through hundreds of documents to find relevant facts that support your case. Just like every other part of the MPT, file documents are created from standard templates and not only is virtually all of the information relevant but it is almost always organized in the same order as the analysis. You do not have to read file documents looking for everything and anything or try to make sense of the information. The organization is there and you just have to know to look for it.

When you read file documents you want to identify not only what facts are relevant but also how they are relevant. The tendency is to read the file and take in the information or make "neutral" notations like circling or underlining. This is a good start but it only identifies that the fact is relevant to a legal issue. You also want to know how that fact fits into your analytical framework. Although file documents are generally organized in order of the main issues, there are often multiple documents per issue or one document contains relevant facts for multiple issues. Therefore, you need a strategy that helps you identify not only what facts are relevant but also how they are relevant.

You can either make a notation in the margins by writing the legal issue or gather facts as you read them and sort them into your already constructed analytical framework. Regardless of whether you make a notation or type facts into your framework, the goal is to build your plan as you work through the documents. Get the most out of every minute so you are not just working quickly but also efficiently.

Your standard approach to reading the MPT material is part of the overall writing process and standard plan. We will explore this in the next chapter.

CHAPTER 4

Standard Approaches to Organizing

Writing is a process and each of the following are distinct and necessary steps:

1. Initiate—lay out the basic framework

2. Identify—what are the specific legal issues

3. Gather—what legal information do you need to answer the question or prove your position, what factual information shows how the legal issues operate?

4. Organize—How do the legal concepts fit together? Build the foundation, organize components, set up the legal mechanisms (definitions, tests, policy, analogies).

5. Explain—how do the client's facts apply. Draft the requested work product.

Just as you have a standard strategy for work through MBE and MEE questions regardless of the subject matter, you also need a standard plan that incorporates the above steps regardless of the MPT problem.

A. "Outlining" for the MPT Is Not the Same as Outlining for Law School Exams

Thus far, I have not used the term "outline" for the MPT and that is for a reason. The analytical framework you build for an MPT is not the same as the outlines you created (or used) for law school exams. Both should be organized so that you can quickly access relevant information but that is where the similarity ends.

When studying for the MBE and MEE, it might be helpful to construct outlines similar to what you did in law school and that is because of the similarity in how those skills are tested. To learn the subject matter tested on law school exams, you must distill an entire semester's worth of material into something more manageable. The resulting outline contains all the rules for the entire subject which you then test out by working through practice questions.

In contrast, the MPT does not test mastery of a particular subject or rule recall. It does not require you to spot issues the same way you do for the MBE and MEE nor do you have to retrieve specific knowledge from your memory such that you need to create a detailed outline. On the MPT, much of the prep work is already done—the task memo tells you what issues to address and the basic structure to follow. Instead of having to identify 2-3 issues from an entire subject area, you are told what the issues are. The material is organized in the order of analysis and the case law analyzes the rules in the same way that you should, including depth of analysis. Every case is on point and contains few (if any) extraneous facts.

So, while outlining for law school is the means by which you will review, synthesize, and learn the course content, "outlining" for the MPT is about setting up an analytical framework such that can execute the task within the time parameters.

B. Constructing an Analytical Framework

The starting point for constructing an analytical framework is to use your time wisely. One of the most common recommendations is to use approximately half of the time allotted to read and plan, and half the time to execute that plan. This is also the most commonly ignored advice because people think, "I only have 90 minutes so I better start writing immediately." This is a mistake because it incorrectly equates writing with thinking. Copying information is not the same as organizing, so do not assume you need to type everything, especially from the library. When you rush to write, you are not in control of the situation and do not trust your ability to set up and execute a plan.

Even after reading the above section, you have likely decided to ignore it and allot 30 minutes to read and organize so you can have 60 minutes to write. You truly believe this is the best way to use your time because you believe you can organize as you write. This is what you did for law school exams. The problem is that this incorrectly assumes the performance expectations on the MPT are the same as the performance expectations on law school exams. It is not.

Even if the MPT expectations were similar to law school exam expectations, trying to think as you write requires you to multi-task. Our brains can only focus on one thing at a time and only 2.5% of the population is legitimately able to multi-task effectively.[1] Before you assume you fit into that exceptional group, let's talk about what multi-tasking requires.

---

[1] https://health.clevelandclinic.org/science-clear-multitasking-doesnt-work/ (last accessed Sept 21, 2022).

Multi-tasking is not really doing multiple tasks at the same time, it is doing individual actions in rapid succession. Your brain has to constantly switch back and forth between tasks, requiring additional energy to focus and refocus. You might be thinking that you have no trouble eating lunch while watching TV or scrolling through social media; you can easily walk while talking to someone or listening to music. These are lower level thinking tasks and that do not require as much active attention. It is much more challenging to effectively multi-task when the tasks are complex and require critical thinking skills such as reading cases, statutes, multiple fact documents, and organizing it a macro and micro level. You cannot copy and paste if you do not know what to copy and where to paste it.

You might still be skeptical and think you are capable of multi-tasking at a high level. I encourage you to try an MPT where you divide your time into 1/3 reading and organizing and 2/3 writing. Perhaps you truly are in that 2% who can effectively multi-task at a high level. Regardless, the experience will be a valuable reminder of what happens when you rush the process. You will be more likely to allow yourself the time you need to read and organize.

Constructing an analytical framework requires you to read the material and set up a plan that you can execute. Although you will need approximately half of your time to do that, it does not have to be 45 minutes up front. You might build the entire framework and then fill it in or you might build and fill one piece at a time. You will do quite a few practice MPTs (7-10) and one reason is so you can try different approaches and figure out which works best.

Start with the 45-45 time division and focus on reading and planning. Again, MPTs are designed from a basic pattern so instead of getting caught up by the surface differences, consciously look for the underlying similarities across MPTs. Trusting yourself and your process is a huge part of doing well on the MPT. Trust that you can take 45 (or even 50!) minutes to read and organize the material. Trust that 45 minutes is enough to execute your plan and complete the tasks.

C. Standard Strategies to Practice

Once you understand the concept of determining your standard approach, you can then work on developing one. This requires more than just doing MPTs, you also need practice strategies.

Large Scale Strategy—Broken MPT

One strategy to fully understanding the difference between writing an outline and building an analytical framework is to do a "broken" MPT. This is a simple yet effective practice strategy that is especially helpful after you have already attempted an MPT or two. It is where you "break" the MPT into distinct components and do each separately with a substantial amount of time in between (at least a few hours or overnight). Because you know you are not going to write the document immediately you know you have to do more than copy static information from the documents and you are not trying to type everything that might be relevant. Instead, you are focused on taking helpful notes to remind you why something is important, how to use it, how issues fit together, etc. When you come back the next day to execute your plan, before you start the clock again, allow yourself a minute or two to refresh the material and quickly skim over any notes.

Small Scale Strategy—Assessing the Steps in Your Process

Oftentimes we only look at the outcome of our efforts and make an assumption about our process. For example, if you get an A on an exam you might assume that everything you did to prepare for it was necessary. And because law students tend to be pretty hard on themselves, if you get a B (or heaven forbid, a C) you go to the other extreme and assume that nothing you did was right or that you are not capable of improving. You then repeat that process, sometimes more intensely but nonetheless the same, without assessing what about it led to the outcome.

Assessing your process means being able to articulate both what you did and why it necessary to produce the final product. It is more than saying, "this is how I always do it," or "this is what the commercial bar prep company said to do."

A building is only as strong as it's foundation and one weak area can cause a major structural issue. The same is true for the MPT. You might have one misstep in your approach or a gap in your thought process that impacts the entire performance. If you can identify and address it, everything else will fall into place. Here are a few small-scale strategies that can have a big impact:

- Roadmap/Introduction—using the task memo introduction for your document is only a time saving strategy if you already have a clear sense of how everything fits together. If you are struggling to organize and write cohesive analysis, it might be helpful to draft your own roadmap/introduction as a way to transition from organizing to writing. Allow yourself 2-3 minutes to pull together your thoughts and write out the steps for the issues.

- Reading Cases—how you read a case can make a huge difference in understanding how to analyze issues. If you feel like it takes you a long time to read cases, try one of these strategies:

  o Identify the issues and read the analysis making only a few notations. Then synthesize the key takeaways and type that into your framework.

- o Do a 30 second skim of a case to identify the main issues and get the overall context and then read it more in depth.

- o Skim all the cases for a big picture context, make a list of the issues, then read each in more detail and fill in the key analytical points.

- o Read the last paragraph of a case first. Oftentimes the court tells you the outcome and basic reason why. Once you know that you know what to look for within the case itself.

- Case Illustrations—if you spend too much time deciding which cases to analogize, try to write one for every case, or write overly in-depth case illustrations, look for internal case illustrations within the cases. These are always concise and on point and a ready-made analogy for your analysis.

Constructing an analytical framework requires creating standard approach and plan. Like any other skill, it comes through deliberate practice and testing within the given parameters. The next chapter discusses standard tools to manage and prioritize your time so you can execute your plan.

CHAPTER 5

Standard Timing Tools

Running out of time is one of the most common obstacles on the MPT. You can have the perfect approach and plan and still not be able to execute within 90 minutes. The MPT is definitely a time-pressured test but most people run out of time because they do not use it wisely. Even when someone has a reliable standard approach plan, they run out of time because they do not manage or prioritize it well. They get caught up in writing the perfect analysis, prioritize document format when there are no specific instructions, attempt to write a case illustration for every issue. Attempting to address the problem of running out of time by trying to work faster assumes that everything you are doing is necessary and that you are actually capable of working faster. Both are incorrect assumptions because neither addresses the real issue of how you are using your time. In order to execute your plan you must manage and prioritize your time.

A. Managing Your Time

Managing your time is about recognizing the appropriate depth of analysis and pacing yourself. Setting a pace lets you know where you are in the process. This helps you to better manage what is in front of you because you know what is ahead of you. Pacing is not about micro-managing every step nor does it depend on the particular MPT. It is about awareness—of your time and where you are in the process.

One strategy for setting your pace is to make time to explicitly transition from planning to executing. Take one minute to "pause and process" and look over the analytical framework you've constructed. Make sure you have the required structural components, identified the major legal issues and confirm they are logically organized, and make note of areas of confusion so that you do not get bogged down but also do not forget to address them later.

Another strategy for pacing yourself is to set reminders with an external timer. Set it for 90 minutes with alarms at 30 minutes left, 15 minutes left, and 5 minutes left. No matter when you start writing, the first alarm will let you know you have 30 minutes left to finish executing your plan. You will automatically recognize where you are in your plan and what you have left to do. You will also naturally pick up the pace a bit and move forward. Then you will hear the second alarm letting you know you have 15 minutes to finish. At the very least, you should be on the last issue/task at this point and you will pick up the pace even more, naturally streamlining the process. The 5 minute alarm lets you know it is time to start wrapping things up. If you have not set up the document components (statement of facts, introduction, headings, etc.) do that now.

These increments help you adjust your pace so that you do not get stuck on one component until it is too late. A 5-minute warning is not very helpful if you lost track of time and are too behind to finish the task. With the incremental signals, even if you have to rush a bit, you still have enough time to recover and finish. You can practice with an external alarm system for a few MPTs but you do not want to rely on it too much because you will not have one during the bar exam. Instead, shift to a manual tracking system by writing down the 30-15-5 minute increments somewhere on the MPT booklet. The act of acknowledging the time is what helps keep you on pace.

You might find that you struggle with one particular aspect and that throws off your overall timing. If you can identify a specific area where you get stuck, you can practice working through it in isolation.

For example, perhaps you spend too much time writing the "perfect" introduction. Try using the factual overview in the task memo as your template. Set a timer for 2-3 minutes and practice writing introductions for MPTs you've already completed. Even though you are already familiar with these MPTs, using them will help you recognize the standard elements of an introduction.

Perhaps you are a "Facts First" person but find yourself spending too much time reading through the file. You want to create conditions that discourage in depth reading while still allowing you to get the factual context. Set a timer for 5 minutes, close your laptop, put away all writing implements, and skim the file. Even if you are not finished with the file at 5 minutes, do not keep reading. Go immediately to the library. Chances are you will discover that you have enough factual context to make sense of the legal issues.

These are just two examples to give you an idea of how you can practice individual components that improve your overall performance.

B. Prioritizing Your Time

In addition to managing your time, you also want to prioritize how you use it. You can only pick up the pace so much and you have to reconcile what you want to do with what you are able to accomplish within 90 minutes. It is not possible to produce a perfect

MPT within 90 minutes so your goal is to produce a professional-ish level document, more like a solid first draft than something that you would actually file with a court, send to a client, or give to the managing partner.

Furthermore, you are not expected to produce a response identical to the samples provided by commercial bar prep companies. These are constructed using the NCBE drafter's point sheets. The point sheets address all points that could be raised in the particular MPT but it is NOT a model answer and you are not expected to address all the issue and points.

The reason the point sheet contains all possible points is so the bar examiners know how to assess performance. Similarly, sample responses created by commercial bar prep companies include all possible points so you can see what could be included and how it should be addressed. Chapter 8 discusses how to use these tools to assess your performance.

Prioritizing your time requires you to make professional judgment calls. You already know how to do this because you have done it on your law school exams, during externships, moot court briefs, and in work environments. Exams have time and word limits and most courts have page limits. You do not write everything available about a rule or make every possible argument; instead you identify what is necessary to establish your case and put forth your strongest reasons supporting that outcome.

Transferring this skill to the MPT is mostly about trusting yourself and what you know:

- MPTs are designed to test a variety of standard legal skills such as fact application, analogical reasoning, and addressing counter arguments.

- You should be able to adequately demonstrate these skills within 90 minutes.

- The MPT material contains all the factual and legal information needed to demonstrate these skills.

From this you can deduce that of the 2-3 main issues raised in the MPT, one will almost always be more straight-forward than the other. The goal is not to show subject mastery but basic skills and you are expected to use the provided problem solving tools, not come up with them on your own. You will be able to recognize the appropriate depth of analysis from the case law and the available facts.

CHAPTER 6

Standard Expectations

As you undoubtedly learned in your legal writing courses, writing is a process that requires you to first organize your ideas, write a draft, and then revise it (often more than once). In the workplace you would not dream of submitting a first draft as your final draft. Skipping steps in the writing process leads to disorganized analysis, missed issues, and awkward grammar in words, sentences, and paragraphs. "If I just had 10 more minutes," might be the most common lament when it comes to the MPT. It is understandable to try and build in time during the MPT to revise and edit. Although you likely cannot speed up enough to have 10 minutes for this, there are strategies you can practice and prepare for that will save you time during the MPT.

A. Standard Components

The point sheet contains explicit expectations for individual MPTs but there are also implicit expectations that are hallmarks of good writing. The bar examiners expect to see these components in an MPT response. Because these are standard writing skills, you can practice them ahead of time.

Document Format

Absent explicit instructions, you only need to set up a general format so the bar examiners know you are following the task instructions. For example, if the task is to draft a memo, include a basic memo heading. If the task is a letter, include a salutation and signature line.

Roadmap/Introduction

A roadmap or introduction tells the reader what to expect in the document. It shows the bar examiner up front that you understand the assigned task and how to address the legal issues. It only has to be 2-3 sentences laying out the main issues and overall outcome. Not only does the roadmap/introduction provide context for the reader, writing it allows you to pull your thoughts together and transition from organizing to writing. You can write your own or copy the factual introduction from the task memo and it is worth practicing both so you can see which approach is most effective for you.

Topic/Thesis Sentences

Every paragraph should start with a sentence that lays out the specific point you will address. A paragraph that starts with only a rule or only facts lacks context and forces the bar examiner to figure out why the information is relevant and how it fits into the rest of the analysis. It might seem like it takes too much time to draft a focused thesis sentence but when you think about what you are going to say the resulting paragraph is more focused and cohesive. The more you practice this, the easier it becomes because you develop the habit of thinking about the connections between concepts instead of just getting thoughts onto the paper.

Direct Reference to Legal Authority

Explicitly refer to legal authority either by an abbreviated citation or integrated into the text. This demonstrates that you are relying on the provided legal sources instead of outside or prior knowledge. As discussed in Chapter 2, citations only need to include the name of the legal authority. Formal citation is not worth the time or effort because the bar examiners are only looking to see that you are using the legal authorities provided, not your format or precision.

Conclusions

In addition to a simple overall conclusion, you should include connection-conclusions for the sub-issues. The overall conclusion can be a general generic sentence that wraps up the analysis: "For the foregoing reasons. . . [outcome on main issues]." The connection-conclusions are what take more practice because you are not just concluding an individual issue but also connecting it to the next issue. This shows the bar examiners that you not only understand individual legal issues but also how they are related to each other and the larger issue.

B. Standard Writing Conventions

Basic writing conventions support the substance of the message and activate meaning so that the text is clear and comprehensible. Bar examiners expect you to know and use the. You should practice using them consistently in your MPTs as a way to revise as you write.

Paragraphing

In addition to your analytical skills, you are also being assessed on organization and logic. The bar examiner will only spend a few minutes reading your entire MPT so use paragraphing to guide them through the document. Think of each paragraph as a step in your logical process and you want each step to be easily identifiable. Get in the habit of starting a new paragraph when you shift from general rules to specific rules or a case illustration, and when you shift from rules to analysis.

Professional Tone

It might seem obvious that you should write in a professional tone but it is often one of the first things abandoned when writing under time pressure. The MPT (and MEE) is not like a law school exam where the goal is to get words on the paper. Avoid contractions and colloquialisms (informal phrases) whenever possible and do not abbreviate unless it is a universally understood term.

Simple Headings

Simple headings help you set up the organizational structure for issues and sub-issues and make it easy for the bar examiner to see that you are addressing the correct issues in a logical order. Unless the MPT has specific instructions, keep headings simple and straightforward, use precise language that states the specific legal issue. If the task is a persuasive one, headings should be concise statements on your position (The Court Should Reach Outcome X Because Legal Standard Met).

Organizational Signals

Organizational signals help guide a reader through a series of ideas and show the connections or sequence of concepts. Consider using numbers, lists, or bullet points when a legal issue has multiple factors or elements. Use transition words and phrases to guide the bar examiner through the analysis (first, next), show relationships between concepts (similarly, in contrast, however), priority and order of importance (primarily, most important).

C. Standard Formulas for Demonstrating Analytical Skills

In addition to practicing standard components and writing conventions ahead of time, you can also develop standard formulas to demonstrate analytical skills such as analogical reasoning, counter arguments and factual ambiguities, and addressing weight of authority. If you develop a standard default approach ahead of time, you will not have to figure this out under pressure during the bar exam.

The following three standard formulas are ways to approach specific components of the basic CREXAC/CREAC analytical framework you learned in your legal writing class.

- A case illustration is part of the rule explanation that sets up a factual comparison in the analysis.

- Address counter arguments and ambiguities within the analysis after establishing your primary position.

- Weight of authority is part of the rule and distinguishes mandatory and persuasive authority.

Analogical Reasoning—Case Illustrations

Every MPT response should contain at least one case illustration because this demonstrates analogical reasoning skills. You know what a case illustration is and you know how to write one. The challenge on the MPT is that you have to think and write fast.

A case illustration is part rule explanation and part application so the 3 + 3 strategy is an effective method for constructing one:

3 Parts from Precedent Case

1. Intro—specific legal principal, use key terms

2. Critical Facts—outcome determinative

3. Reasoning—basis for the outcome

3 Parts from Present Circumstances

1. Connect—relationship to precedent

2. Critical Facts—explain how facts are similar/ different from precedent

3. Conclusion—legal outcome, use key terms

Example:

Precedent Case:

1. Intro—In *Preston v. George*, the court addressed the issue of whether an individual is "readily identifiable" even when a person's face is obscured.

2. Critical facts—In that case, a professional skier's face was obscured by his ski helmet and neither his name nor bib number was visible. However, he wore a distinctive purple and gold ski suit.

3. Reasoning—The court stated that the question is not whether one can recognize an individual's features but whether one can identify the specific individual. Because the suit's color scheme and design were unique to the skier, the court held that this was sufficient to be readily identifiable. *Preston*.

Present Circumstances:

1. Connect—Our case is different from *Preston*.

2. Critical Facts—Unlike the distinctive ski suit in *Preston*, the photo here depicts the athlete wearing the standard team uniform, the same one every player wears. Although the player's number is unique, the cloud of dust obscuring his face also covers one of the numbers on his uniform. The team has had the same uniform for 25 years so the photo could depict any number of current or former players.

3. Reasoning—Unlike the purple and gold ski suit, nothing about the athlete here is distinguishable or unique, thus he is not readily identifiable.

Counter Arguments and Ambiguities

A second default formula to practice is counter analysis and ambiguities. Every MPT task memo has explicit instructions to resolve or address counter analysis/arguments so you know the bar examiners expect you to demonstrate this skill. However, do not fall into the trap of thinking there is a counter for every issue. If the task is predictive, identify plausible weaknesses or alternative interpretations. If the task is persuasive, look for plausible challenges to your position.

Similar to counter analysis are factual and legal ambiguities but a bit more subtle in how they present. Every MPT has facts and law that are irrelevant do not dismiss something simply because it does not change the outcome of your reasoning. Instead, learn to recognize the difference between irrelevant and ambiguous. Something is irrelevant only if it is inapplicable to the issue and there is no legal or factual connection. Something is ambiguous if it is susceptible to more than one interpretation but does not ultimately change the outcome of your position or prediction.

If it is ambiguous, address both potential interpretations and explain which is more likely. The default formula for addressing counter analysis and ambiguities is Address-Reconcile-Return.

- Address—address and specifically identify the potential conflict and establish the specific rule (Although. . . or Even though. . .).

- Reconcile—reconcile the conflict/weakness by explaining how your facts are distinguishable from precedent facts, or accurately explaining how the rule works (Here. . . Because. . .).

- Return—return back to position by concluding on legal issue (Therefore. . .).

Example of Formula Components:

- Address—Even though the length of time in our case is less than in the precedent, our client's grandparents qualify as parents.

- Reconcile—Here, the client's grandparents took over the day-to-day parenting decisions and provided both personal and financial support for substantial periods of time because the parents were in an out of prison and rehab. If our client's grandparents had not taken them in, she and her sibling and would not have been able to take care of or support themselves.

- Return—Therefore, the length of time does not detract from establishing a grandmother is a parent under in *loco parentis*.

Example in Paragraph Form:

Although Matthew attempted to make the house individual property by only putting his name on the deed, this was ineffective.

Under the statute, marital property is property accumulated during the marriage regardless of whether title held individually or jointly. Here, the date on the deed is August 8, 2012, well after the parties established their common law marriage. Therefore, the house is marital property and subject to equitable distribution.

Weight of Authority

Sometimes the MPT library will contain persuasive legal authority either from another jurisdiction (neighboring states of Olympia or Columbia) or as common law that has since been codified and there is no case law to interpret the statute. When the library contains persuasive legal authority it is a signal that you are being tested not just on your ability to apply the substance of that legal source but also your understanding of how to use it. Develop a default formula so you can practice addressing the weight of authority and how it fits into the legal analysis: acknowledging the legal source is not binding but that it is consistent with how a Franklin court would interpret the matter.

Examples:

This is an issue of first impression in Franklin so there is no binding authority. However, Columbia/Olympia courts have addressed the issue and although only persuasive, it is instructive on how a Franklin court would rule.

The common law has since been codified. Although not binding, the prior case law is consistent with the legislative intent and instructive on how a court would interpret the statute.

D. What Not to Do

Unless specifically directed, some things do not demonstrate any of the tested skills so there is no explicit or implicit expectation. You should not include them "just in case" or for extra credit because the bar examiners may not consider anything outside of the official point sheet. In fact, including them could negatively impact your score because it took time and effort away from what actually is on the point sheet.

Citing to the File

Unlike legal material, you cannot get factual information from an outside source or prior knowledge. Using specific facts in the analysis shows you are relying on the material. It is acceptable to reference a file document if it flows into the analysis but make sure to include specific facts. Mentioning a file document is not a substitute for factual analysis.

Statement of Facts

Unless instructed to do so, writing a statement of facts will likely lower your score because you ignored the task memo instructions saying do not include it. Even when a task memo instructs you to include a statement of facts, it is often limited to a "brief statement of salient facts." This means a short paragraph giving a general overview. Instead of writing it first, write it in the last 1-2 minutes after you are familiar enough with the facts to be able to quickly summarize the situation.

Over-Formatting

Show that you understand the basic task but keep the formatting simple—standard memo heading, letter salutation, etc. Including things like letterhead and detailed headings do not demonstrate any skills that are not already demonstrated through other means.

CHAPTER 7

Standard Strategies to Practice

There is no question you will practice several (7-10) MPTs but doing an MPT because it is assigned by commercial bar prep or because you know you are supposed to will not improve your skills or adequately prepare you for the bar exam. You want to understand when, how, and what to practice.

Those using a commercial bar prep program should start with the MPTs already provided and if you do not have access to a full service commercial bar prep program, you can find plenty of MPTs on the NCBE website.

- Most recent 5 years—free summaries of issues and tasks, individual MPTs and point sheets available for purchase ($20/exam).

- 6-10 years old—20 free MPTs and point sheets.

Do not assume that the most recent MPTs are the best or immediately purchase five years' worth of MPTs. Start with the resources you already have available.

A. When and How to Practice

Most commercial bar prep companies schedule several MPT early in bar prep and then space them regularly throughout, including a full practice exam. The reason for this is so you can first get familiar with the MPT and start to develop an approach, then build on your strengths and address weaknesses, and finally test your process for overall performance. Ultimately, you want to know why your process works beyond "commercial bar prep said to do it."

The first stage practice is about familiarizing yourself with the MPT and developing a reliable approach. This requires you to work through at least 3 MPTs in pretty close succession early in bar prep. You should see marked improvement by the third MPT and feel pretty confident in your approach, and you should also be able pinpoint specific weaknesses or areas where you are struggling.

Once you have a basic approach, you can then improve on it by addressing weak areas, experimenting with different strategies and streamlining the overall process. You should do 3-4 more MPTs by early July and do not expect every MPT to go well. You want to make mistakes and address them now instead of during the bar exam. For example, you decide to try typing facts from the file directly into your analytical framework instead of making notes in the MPT. The result is that you had too much information on the page and it took longer organize how you incorporated facts into the analysis. This MPT was not a disaster or a waste of time because not only have you learned what works for you but you understand why. You also want to test your approach under different circumstances. See the "What to Practice" section for details.

In the last few weeks before the bar exam you will work through 2-3 MPTs to keep your skills fresh and perhaps make a few minor tweaks. If you have not yet practiced doing 2 MPTs in 3 hours, now is the time for that. If you only practice one MPT at a time, it is easy to stop at 90 minutes. Not only do you want to practice managing your time but it is a different experience to work intensely non-stop for 3 hours.

B. What to Practice

Most bar prep guides categorize MPTs by subject and individual task and it makes it seem like every MPT is different. You have read enough of this book to know that MPTs are based on standard patterns and formulas which means you should look beyond "opinion letter," or "criminal law," and identify categories of tasks and skills.

There are two categories of tasks: basic and specialized. Basic tasks are memos, opinion letters, briefs, demand letters. Specialized tasks are transactional drafting, persuasive drafting, and multi-task (draft two different documents). The tasks do have a basic skill component, but they are more the vehicle for testing legal analysis skills.

Basic Tasks

Basic tasks are both familiar to most people and have straightforward formats. But just because you may be familiar and comfortable with the particular task does not mean the MPT itself is simple. Oftentimes a basic task is paired with a more complex legal analysis skill.

Memos are the most basic predictive task and require an objective analysis advising the managing attorney on the merits of civil, criminal, or administrative claims or issues.

Opinion letters are similar to the objective analysis of a memo and the difference is that instead of writing to a supervising attorney, you are writing directly to the client and explaining your professional assessment of the likelihood of success on claims.

Briefs are the most basic persuasive task and require you to draft the argument section of a trial or appellate court case. The main legal objectives will be laid out in task memo and you must make the specific arguments in support of those objectives.

Demand letters are similar to briefs in that you are advocating for a certain outcome but a demand letter is at the pre-litigation stage so the goal is slightly different. You are trying to persuade the recipient (usually the opposing party) that not only is your legal position correct but that it is in their best interest to agree to your specific demands.

Specialized Tasks

Specialized tasks are not necessarily complex or tricky but not everyone is familiar with them which is why they will almost always include specific instructions or formatting guidance.

Transactional drafting is a predictive task with two components: (1) draft (or re-draft) select provisions of a document such as a contract, arbitration provision, liability waiver, or corporate policy/procedure, and (2) explain how the provisions comply with relevant legal requirements while also meeting the client's expressed goals.

Persuasive drafting is sort of a hybrid of transactional drafting and brief because there is a specific template to follow and you are advocating for a certain position or outcome. Examples include a closing argument, document persuading legislators to vote in favor of legislation, proposed findings of fact and conclusions of law.

The multi-task MPT is one where you must draft two distinct documents on a related issue. One is almost always predictive and the other is persuasive and one will require more in-depth analysis which means you must prioritize which task will take longer and manage time accordingly.

Legal Analysis Skills

Within the type of task or document format, the MPT also tests your legal analysis skills. Legal analysis skills fall into two categories: sources of authority and decision-making or prioritizing. Sources of legal authority are common law synthesis, statutory interpretation, and regulatory interpretation. Decision-making or prioritizing MPTs include factors analysis and organizational decisions.

Sources of Authority

Common law synthesis is the most basic analytical skill because the legal authority is all case law. The skill tested is being able to extract the legal principle from each case and identify the common legal theme. Look for how cases are related because this connection is the analytical framework.

Statutory interpretation and regulatory interpretation MPTs are similar in that the language is the starting point for analysis but the structure is not one you can follow to organize your analysis. However, the analysis is not the same. Statutes are enacted by legislatures and regulate behavior while regulations are rules set by agencies that govern how statutes are enforced. Regulations are more detailed that statutes. Statutory analysis is what the rule is and what it means while regulatory analysis is how the law works and what actions someone should or should not take.

Professional responsibility/ethics is the only substantive MPT that is worth noting and only because it is a hybrid of statutory and regulatory interpretation. The code of professional conduct (almost always identical to the ABA Model Rules) regulates behavior and the actions one should or should not take. Professional responsibility MPTs include the code, comments, ethics opinions, and court opinions. Comments address who the rules apply to and provide guidance on how to comply. Ethics opinions are non-binding guidance on how the rules apply, and court opinions address both how the rules apply and how to analyze any overlapping legal issues.

Decision-Making and Prioritizing

If you do not know to look for decision-making and prioritizing as an explicit legal analysis skill, you will waste valuable time being confused and second-guessing yourself. An MPT that tests decision-making skills does not seem to have a clear structure or hierarchy and oftentimes there are no specific formatting guidelines. It is easy to get bogged down trying to figure out the "right" way to organize the analysis. Although there is usually a general hierarchy, the specific legal issues are inter-connected and often overlap each other.

The most straightforward example of this skill is a factors analysis test. Factors are circumstances to be considered in reaching an outcome. It is a balancing test where you must examine each factor and balance the interests to reach a just result. Sometimes one factor might carry more weight than others but it is not outcome determinative by itself. Part of the legal analysis is organizing how to address each factor.

One of the most common mistakes people make is to look at the task memo or format document for help in prioritizing and making analytical decisions. These are analytical organization decisions so guidance comes from the legal sources.

C. Standard MPTs to Practice

Although there are only two types of basic MPT tasks— predictive and persuasive—there are a few standard MPT skills that are commonly tested. These include basic tasks, specialized tasks, sources of legal authority, and decision-making and prioritizing.

Basic Tasks—Memo, opinion letters, briefs, and demand letters.

Memos

Kline v. State of Franklin (Oct 20)

In re Zimmer Farms (July 17)

In re Harrison (Feb 15)

State of Franklin v. Soper (July 12)

Opinion Letters

In re Canyon Gate Property Owners Association (July 21)

In re Bryan Carr (July 15)

In re Franklin Aces (July 15)

In re WPE Property Development, Inc. (Feb 12)

Briefs

State of Franklin v. Clegane (Feb 18)

In re Rowan (Feb 14)

Monroe v. Franklin Flags Amusement Park (July 13)

In re Hammond (July 10)

Demand Letters

Miller v. Trapp (Feb 16)

In re Community General Hospital (Feb 16)

In re Linda Duram (July 13)

In re City of Bluewater (July 09) *response to a demand letter*

Glickman v. Phoenix Cycles, Inc. (Feb 07)

Specialized Tasks—Transactional drafting, persuasive drafting, and multi task (ex: memo and a closing argument).

Transactional Drafting

Rugby Owners and Players Association (July 18)

In re Peterson Engineering Consultants (July 14)

Palindrome Recording Contract (July 13)

In re Field Hogs (July 11)

Logan v. Rios (Feb 10)

In re Velocity Park (Feb 08)

Persuasive Drafting (non-brief)

In re Eli Doran (Feb 20)

In re Guardianship of Henry King (Feb 17)

Franklin Resale Royalties Legislation (Feb 12)

Multi-Task

Miller v. Trapp (Feb 16)

Butler v. Hill (Feb 11)

Williams v. A-1 Automotive Center (July 08)

Sources of Legal Authority—Common law synthesis, statutory interpretation, regulatory interpretation, and interpretation professional code of conduct.

Common Law Synthesis

In re Eli Doran (Feb 20)

Miller v. Trapp (Feb 16)

In re Magnolia County (Feb 11)

Monroe v. Franklin Flags Amusement Park (July 13)

In re Clarke Corporation (July 05)

Statutory Interpretation

In re Zimmer Farm (July 18)

Peek et al v. Doris Stern Allied Behavioral Health Services (July 17)

In re Anderson (Feb 16)

Jackson v. Franklin Sports Gazette (July 09)

Regulatory Interpretation

In re Community General Hospital—HIPAA (Feb 15)

In re Linda Duram—FMLA (Feb 14)

City of Ontario (July 10)

Glickman v. Phoenix Cycles—FMLA (Feb 07)

Hybrid—Professional Code of Conduct

Downey v. Achilles Medical Device Company (Feb 20)

In re Ace Chemical (Feb 17)

In re Kay Struckman (July 14)

In re Wendy Martel (Feb 13)

In re Hammond (July 10)

Parker v. Essex Productions (July 06)

Decision-Making & Prioritizing—Factors analysis and organizational decisions.

Factors Analysis

Winston v. Franklin T-Shirts, Inc. (July 21)

Nash v. Franklin Department of Revenue (July 16)

In re Rowan (July 14)

In re Marian Bonner (July 04)

Organizational Decisions

Fun4Kids Terms of Service Agreement (July 20)

In re Hastings (Feb 15)

In re Barbara Whirley (July 14)

In re Wendy Martel (Feb 13)

CHAPTER 8

Standard Strategies for Assessing Process and Skills

A. The Importance of Self-Assessment

Although commercial bar prep companies will grade some of your MPTs (and essays), you are also expected to do quite a bit of self-assessment and self-grading. Assessment is not the same thing as grading: assessment focuses on the process while grading is about performance. You need both because a grade on your performance is the starting point for assessing the process and the process is what leads to the performance. Assessment is similar to feedback you likely received from your legal writing professor—explanations of strengths and weaknesses and how to address them or transfer it to another issue. Commercial bar prep companies will not assess your process because they do not have a mechanism for seeing what you did that led to the finished product. Even though you might not realize it, you have the ability to self-assess your writing process and work product. Being able to do this yourself instead of relying on external feedback not only improves your ability to do it but also develops confidence in your own abilities.

It is difficult to accurately self-assess your process or grade your performance without some guidance. You have several assessment and grading tools for the MPT.

B. Assess the Skills That Are Tested

Task Memo

Read the task memo again—what were you asked to do? How were you asked to do it?

Compare to your response—did you resolve the issues exactly as instructed?

Key Components

Do you have an introduction that sets up a roadmap and provides context?

Did you include one case illustration?

Does every paragraph start with a topic sentence?

- Highlight the first sentence of every paragraph—does it clearly identify the topic?

Do you use transition words/phrases that signal how the components fit together?

Are your paragraphs a reasonable length and convey one idea?

Analysis

Did you use specific facts in your analysis?

- Go through your response and highlight specific facts used.

- Now highlight those facts in the file.

- Identify facts in the file not used in your response.

- The more unused facts, the more incomplete your analysis.

C. Assess Your Process

Time Management

What was your time management plan? How well did you follow it?

Did you run out of time?

- Spend too much time on the first issue?
- Spend too much time reading the file?
- Spend too much time on unnecessary components?
- Did you write too many rules?

Pressure Management

Were you confused? Did you get lost? Why?

How did you resolve issues of confusion?

Identify 2-3 tangible things you did well.

Identify 2-3 actions to improve your performance on the next MPT.

A detailed assessment checklist is at the end of the chapter.

D. How to Use the Assessment and Grading Tools

You have several grading tools to help you assess your progress and grade your performance on the MPT: the drafter's point sheet, commercial bar company sample responses, and jurisdiction released responses. No single tool is enough on its own. You can more accurately self-assess and grade if you use them together. The drafter's point sheet identifies minimum and above average expectations, commercial bar company sample responses are best for structure and organization, and released responses show you a somewhat realistic expectation under exam conditions.

Drafter's Point Sheet

Always use the drafters point sheet because it is what the bar examiners use to grade your MPT. It should be your primary source for self-assessment but although it is called a point sheet, the name is a misnomer. The point sheet is a narrative description of what the MPT problem contains and of issues to be addressed, how an examinee might address them, as well as what should not be addressed. There are no points or percentage weights assigned (unlike the MEE answer analyses which suggest percentages for each issue) but it does contain helpful guidance for how to distinguish the quality of responses.

Although guidance is specific for each MPT, like most assessment criteria, it falls into two general categories—basic instructional skills and higher order critical thinking skills.

Basic instructional skills set minimum expectations such as what you should or should not include or what legal standards must be addressed. Skills that distinguish an above average response might include words like "perceptive," and "excellent" that tell the bar examiners they should not expect most examinees to address the particular point or issue because it tests a higher level critical thinking skill.

When you go through the drafter's point sheets, go beyond simply looking at whether you addressed the listed issue. Identify and categorize the basic instructional skills and the critical thinking skills and determine whether you met minimum expectations or demonstrated critical thinking skills.

Commercial Bar Prep Company Sample Responses

The drafter's point sheets usually identify all relevant facts and then lay out all the legal issues to address so although you know what facts to use, you also need to see how the facts and rules work together. Commercial bar prep companies draft sample MPT responses that are basically the point sheet in narrative form. It is helpful for assessing structure and organization but not as much for the substantive quality of analysis. The commercial bar prep companies make it clear that the sample responses are not model responses and should not be used as such.

The response comparison chart at the end of this chapter is a helpful tool for assessing your response with the sample response as it gives you a side by side comparison of organization, rules, and facts used. Although you should pay attention to any issues you missed or did not fully address, also take note of whether you over analyzed or discussed an issue not addressed in the sample response. This will show you places where you can better manage time and priorities.

Jurisdiction Released Responses

Some jurisdictions like California, Georgia, Maryland, New York, Ohio, and Texas publish released essay and MPT responses as examples of what the best response was for that particular exam. Before you rush to compare these released responses to your MPTs, first assess the released response using the drafter's point sheet or, if available, the commercial bar prep sample. You should notice that the released response is not identical to the drafter's point sheet or the sample response. It will not address every point or fully analyze every issue, it might have a different organizational structure, or reach different outcomes, etc.

Next, compare released responses across jurisdictions and look for similarities as well as differences. The responses will not be identical but what seems to be a standard indicator of excellence? What you should take away from this exercise is that an excellent response is not perfect and there is more than one way to write an excellent response.

When you compare your response to the released response, look for the standard indicators of excellence and while you should not count every difference as a negative, do not ignore them either. Remember that you are looking at the best response and because scoring is curved, many other responses will receive that same top score. Furthermore, although you can aim to be the best, you do not need to earn the best score to pass the bar exam.

If there is something in the released response that especially stands out and you want to include it in your MPT responses, take a few minutes to figure out if and how it fits into your process. Just as you do not do something because commercial bar prep said to do it or that's what you've always done, you don't do something simply because you saw it in the released response.

E. MPT Self-Assessment

Performance Assessment: Structure, Style, Substance

☐ Overall look is a professional document.

☐ Tone is professional: respectful, no colloquialisms, no abbreviations.

☐ Tone is confident and direct: clear outcomes, answers questions from task memo.

☐ Writing style is clear and concise: gets to the point, not rambling and difficult to follow.

    ☐ Avoids use of passive voice.

    ☐ Not redundant.

    ☐ Avoids pretentious, overly formalistic, and outdated legalisms.

☐ Answers only the legal questions asked.

☐ Follows structure and format directions.

☐ Macro organization makes sense and has a logical flow.

☐ 2-3 sentence intro/roadmap to provide context for the bar examiner.

☐ Headings (if appropriate) and transitional phrases that make it easy for bar examiner to see connections.

☐ Effective use of paragraphing to break up information into manageable chunks.

☐ Starts every paragraph with a thesis sentence that puts law and/or facts in context.

☐ Correctly identifies the issues raised.

☐ Recognizes "tell" from "prove" issues and addresses appropriate depth of analysis.

☐ Rule statements are correct, concise, complete.

☐ Focused and accurate rule explanations using key language.

☐ Uses parallel rule language in the analysis to show law + fact connection.

☐ References every document in the library.

☐ Analysis incorporates specific facts from every document in the file.

☐ Includes at least one case example with direct fact-to-fact comparison/contrast.

☐ Addresses and reconciles ambiguous facts (instead of ignoring).

F. Process Assessment—Strategy and Approach

- Identify 2-3 things you did well.

- Identify 2-3 things that didn't go well.

- What is your default approach (as of now) and why?

- What is your time management plan: reading, writing, organizing, and why?

- Compared to your first (or most recent), where have you improved the most?

- Identify 2-3 specific things you can do to improve efficiency (not faster but smarter).

- On a scale of 1-6, what score would you give yourself and why? *Guidance: 3—slightly below avg, 4—slightly above avg.*

G. MPT Answer Comparison Chart

This chart is only a template. You may need to add more spaces.

	My Response	Sample Response
Task Format		
Main Legal Issues		
Heading 1		
Rule(s) Used		
Facts Used		
Heading 2		
Rule(s) Used		
Facts Used		
Heading 3		

H. Assessment Questions

- Did your answer follow the directions of the task memo explicitly?

- Does the overall organization and order of your answer follow that of the sample response? If not, what is different and does your response still follow a logical legal hierarchy?

- Is the breakdown of any sub-issues (e.g., rules with multiple elements) in your answer similar to that of the sample answer?

- Does your answer reference every legal authority from the Library, and include the specific facts used in the sample answer? If not, what is missing and did it lead to you missing an issue, is there a gap in analysis, or conclusory analysis?

CHAPTER 9

Standard Mistakes and Misconceptions

A. Standard Mistakes (and How to Avoid Them)

Work Product Related

Not using all the documents in the library and/or file. This mistake is connected to the myth sometimes a document is irrelevant and you should ignore it. On the contrary, every document is relevant to the task and the legal issues. You might not use every detail in a document but you <u>will</u> use every document in your response. If you are not sure how something is relevant to the task or legal issues, address it at the very end by adding a "also relevant to the situation is [document name]" paragraph where you describe the particular document in a few sentences.

Thinking formatting is the same thing as organizing. As discussed in Chapter 2, the bar examiners only spend a few minutes per MPT and scoring is relative. They expect to see cohesive and logical analysis, not firm letterhead, full citations, detailed headings and sub-headings, nor long conclusions repeating what you already said.

Creating abbreviations that have no clear meaning. Creating specialized abbreviations, especially acronyms detracts from clarity which can negatively impact your overall score. For example, if the client is University General Hospital, abbreviating it to "UGH" has no meaning attached to it and it detracts from the name of the client. Instead of a vague abbreviation, use a word that has meaning and is obvious who you are referring to. For example, say "Hospital" or "University General." This also goes for statutes and regulations when discussing them within the analysis. Do not just state the provision section without establishing what the provision addresses. For example, instead of, "Calvin does not have jurisdiction under § 42.01 but he does under § 42.03," say, "Calvin does not have general jurisdiction under § 42.01 but he does have specific jurisdiction under § 42.03." Including the key terms provides level of clarity the bar examiners expect.

Note—there are three exceptions to abbreviating: you may abbreviate a statute name (UCC instead of Uniform Commercial Code), you may use commonly known abbreviations (HIPAA, FMLA, etc.), and if the abbreviation is used within the MPT.

Time-Related

Time management is one of the skills the MPT tests which means you must manage your time under pressure. You have to think and write fast but if you are unable to complete an MPT, the solution is not just simply trying to increase your speed.

Instead of working faster, using surface level short cuts (abbreviating words), or giving up because you think you're just slower than everyone else, evaluate your work to figure out why you are running out of time.

Did you spend too much time on formatting? Do you spend too much time copying every rule from the library and not have enough time for analysis? Copying rules is not a skill but explaining how they apply to the facts is. When you are focused on copying legal information it is easy to miss how the rules operate and then you have to spend time figuring this out.

Even though there are no points to win or lose (see myths below), it makes sense to address as many legal and factual points as you can. Let's say you need to address 2/3 of the legal and factual points laid out in the drafters' point sheet. You want to spread that out over all the issues, not by addressing everything in the first issue while barely getting any in the second. There might be three cases you could analogize but start with one and if you have time, come back and include additional analogies.

One of the worst time related mistakes is going over time when practicing. Even if you make a note afterwards of how much you completed in 90 minutes, this sends the signal to your brain that everything you are doing in that 90 minutes is absolutely necessary and there is no incentive to change. Even if you tell yourself you will stick to 90 minutes, your brain knows you won't follow through and you will give yourself more time. This is a bad habit that will hurt you when it matters most—on the actual exam. You can kid yourself and say that you will stick to 90 minutes when it matters but your brain does not know how to complete a 90 minute MPT. You have not learned to manage your time so when you get both MPTs and have 3 hours to complete them, you wind up borrowing time from the second MPT.

If you needed 95 minutes to complete one MPT, how will you complete the second one in 85 minutes? This is a 10 minute differential, which is a lot of time in MPT terms (it would be the equivalent of not addressing an entire issue). Rationalizing that you will get a better score on one to balance out the lower score on the other is also a bad mistake because—you guessed it—this is relative grading. How can you guarantee that you will get a high enough score on the first MPT to offset what is likely to be a below average score on the second? This is not a risk worth taking, especially because it is one you can avoid.

B. Standard Misconceptions

Tricks and Hidden Issues

People like to point to the language in the instructions that says, "may include some facts that are not relevant," and "may also include some authorities that are not relevant," to perpetuate the myth that some documents are included to trick you. The only trick is the one you play on yourself by overthinking and making the MPT more difficult than it actually is. As discussed in Chapter 1, the bar exam is called a standardized test because it conforms to—you guessed it—certain standards. Regardless of what you think of the NCBE and standardized testing as a whole, the NCBE follows best practices for standardized tests which includes consistency. In other words, every MPT problem would contain an irrelevant document. There has never been an MPT where an entire document—file or library—has been unnecessary to the task or issues. There might be details within a document that are not relevant but never the entire document.

As much as people despise the bar exam, unlike law school exams which test subject mastery, the bar exam tests minimum competency. Where a law school professor might include subtle or hidden issues as a way to differentiate students, this is not what the MPT seeks to do instead, it presents fairly straightforward legal issues and basic legal tasks. An MPT might have one or two small nuanced issues but not addressing these issues likely would not impact your score. This is all to say, do not look for tricks or hidden issues.

Picking Up and Losing Points

There are no points to pick up or lose because the MPT is graded on a relative curve (usually range of 1-6) based on holistic assessment. It is not merit or standards based grading where your score is determined by how many points you get overall. The bar examiners spend no more than a few minutes per MPT response and assign it a score based on how it compares to other responses. They will not take points off if you reach the wrong conclusion just as they will not give you points for reaching the correct conclusion. I discussed this briefly in Chapter 1 but the bar examiners do not assess an MPT as passing or failing. Your goal should not be to try and get a particular score but to produce work product that responds to the questions asked with analysis that is organized and logical.

Not Trusting Yourself

This might be the last misconception I address but it the most important point in the book. You have been preparing for the bar exam for at least the last three years, learned the skills it tests, and most likely used them in the real world. Why *wouldn't* you trust yourself?

Would you advise a client to panic or tell a friend they're stupid for not immediately knowing how to do something? Of course not. So, why would you say those things to yourself? The words we say to ourselves matter. Trust yourself and your process.